FAVORED NOT FORGOTTEN

LEADER GUIDE

ADAM MCCAIN AND DR. SCOTT SILVERII

Copyright

© 2020 by Dr. Scott Silverii and Adam McCain

Five Stones Press, Dallas, Texas www.fivestonesu.com

All rights reserved. No part of this publication may be reproduced, stored in a retrieval system, or transmitted in any form or by any means—electronic, mechanical, photocopy, recording, or any other—except for brief quotations in printed reviews, without the prior permission of the publisher.

Most Scripture quotations are from the Holy Bible: New King James Version®. NKJV®. Copyright © 1982 by Thomas Nelson, Inc. Used by permission. All rights reserved.

Other versions used include: NASB - New American Standard Bible®, Copyright © 1960, 1962, 1963, 1968, 1971, 1972, 1973, 1975, 1977, 1995 by The Lockman Foundation.

NIV - The Holy Bible, New International Version® NIV® Copyright © 1973, 1978, 1984 by International Bible Society® Used by permission. All rights reserved worldwide.

NET - New English Translation® NET® Copyright © 1996-2006 by Biblical Studies Press, L.L.C. All rights reserved.

KJV - King James Version, Authorized King James Version, Public Domain.

99 01 435769 987123 / 001 / 76430205

Printed in the United States of America

And David shepherded them with integrity of heart;

with skillful hands he led them.

Psalm 78:72

Small Group Guidelines

All small group study groups need to be safe places to share private life issues. This is the only way for them to be successful and promote personal growth of each member. The Small Group Covenant Guidelines ensure this and should be read with the group at the first meeting and reviewed at the beginning of every meeting thereafter.

Small Group Guidelines:

1. Each person should keep their focus on their own thoughts and feelings.

2. Each person is free to express feelings without interruption. Mutual respect is shown when we value the opinions of others [even when we disagree] and are careful to never belittle or embarrass another.

3. We are here to support one another. We are not here to fix one another.

4. Anonymity and confidentiality are basic requirements. Each person should feel safe to share their challenges, failures and successes. Therefore, what is shared in the group stays in the group. Nothing discussed should be repeated outside the group. *The only exception is if someone threatens to harm themselves or others.

5. This is an adults only group.

Small Group Covenant

Every group should agree to some common values upon which the group meetings will be based. Discuss these guidelines to lay that foundation and review them periodically to ensure that the group is handled with integrity and fidelity. Modify and add anything that will make your group work better.

I agree to the following values:

Attendance: To give priority to the group meetings and call if you will be absent or late.

Safe Environment: This will be a safe place where women can be heard and feel respected [no quick answers, snap judgements, or simple fixes]

Confidentiality: Everything is kept strictly confidential and within the group.

Conflicts: To resolve disagreements quickly and biblically according to the principles in Matthew 18:15-17 and to not have any part in gossip.

Spiritual Health: To give the group members permission to speak into my life and to help me move forward in spiritual health and wholeness of thoughts, feelings, and actions.

Limit our Freedom: To not serve or consume alcohol during small group meetings or events.

Welcome Newcomers: To invite friends who might benefit from this study and welcome newcomers.

Build Relationships: To get to know the other members of the group and pray for them regularly.

Other:

WE HAVE ALSO DISCUSSED AND AGREED TO THE FOLLOWING:

Starting Time:

Ending Time:

Childcare:

Suggestions for Success

Thank you for facilitating your group! The following proven suggestions will help you further the success of your group.

Notes for small group facilitators:

Prior to the First Meeting

- Prior to the first meeting, contact all your small group members. Welcome them and remind them of meeting date, time and place. Encourage them to read the chapters that will be discussed at the first group meeting.

- Leaders may also wish to access the Favored Not Forgotten website's video teaching series that accompany each of the 8 sessions. This is located at https://www.favorednotforgotten.com/

At Every Meeting

- Begin and end with prayer. Inviting Jesus into the meeting at the start is vital. Because group members will be revealing vulnerable aspects of their lives, closing with prayer is equally important, asking God to protect their hearts and minds and to help them grow in grace and in the knowledge of Him.

- You should read over the group guidelines before each meeting.

First Meeting - Week 1

- After opening prayer [after this meeting, encourage the opening prayer to be led by other group members], read the small group covenant and the group guidelines. You and each member should sign the covenant.

Suggestions for Success

- Be respectful of the members' schedules. Start on time and end on time.

- Relax and enjoy the group. You are here to facilitate, help the group run smoothly. You are not a counselor. You are working on you. Don't monopolize the conversation.

- Stay on the material. Don't venture off on topics not connected to this study. Having said that, the curriculum is a "guide" so don't feel you have to answer every question in every section. This is not a race to the finish, but a time to examine self, share and support, and let God work in the lives of each member as an individual and the group as a collective unit. Prayerfully read over the material beforehand and choose one or two of the discussion items you feel are most important to get to and lead with that if you feel time is short.

- Group meeting should last no more than 90 minutes.

- Close the group after the second week. Group members will struggle to feel safe if fresh faces show up every week.

- Suggested group size is 6 to 8. Anything larger will not allow for everyone to share answers.

- Assure group members that it's okay to not answer a question. There is no pressure. Members will share when they feel safe. Give the freedom to share, but don't demand that they do. More conversation will happen when people don't feel pressured to speak. Get comfortable with silence, let the members have a couple of minutes to think through on their answer. Simple responses to someone who shares are "thanks" or "great answer," "thanks for sharing." Then, "would someone else like to add anything"?

- Childcare can be tricky. Because this is not a couples' group, it may not be an issue; however, it should be worked out before the need arises. If necessity dictates that several ladies must bring their children, one way to handle this is hiring a sitter to watch all the children in another area of the meeting place. Discuss and decide how this will work at the first meeting.

Introduction

Favored Not Forgotten: Embrace the Season, Thrive in Obscurity, Activate Your Purpose Leader's Guide

Based on the *Favored Not Forgotten: Embrace the Season, Thrive in Obscurity, Activate Your Purpose* book by Dr. Scott Silverii & Adam McCain, this leader's guide is designed as a companion for the book, student workbook and video series. *Favored Not Forgotten* is available in book and workbooks for individuals, small groups and divorce care.

Welcome to the **Favored Not Forgotten Leader's Guide.** We are so proud of you for taking the necessary steps to care for yourself. This is no time to feel guilty about making sure you are okay. We want you to know that you'll be better than okay because you'll be making tough decisions based on biblical advice.

This workbook, just like the book, relies on God's Word for guiding us through darkness and into the light. Allow this workbook to help reinforce what it is that the pages of Favored Not Forgotten have spoken into your life.

In addition to the book and this workbook, we've developed a video series to help walk you through topics that might be better received from a trusted friend or mentor. This combination of resources will provide you with practical, biblically based guidelines, insightful discussions, and life-changing applications.

As you prepare for the first session, we want to encourage you in three areas:

- **First – *Be committed.*** If you are committed to God first, you can survive anything and live a blessed life in His light.

- **Second – *Be Bold.*** Some of the discussion questions may challenge you to talk about important issues. It's normal to feel some resistance when you feel as though you've been hurt or disappointed. However, it's important to acknowledge what's really going on in your heart and mind.

- **Third – *Focus on what you can do.*** Some discussion questions may present an opportunity to be critical of yourself and others. There will be times when you can honestly say how you feel about important issues. But the key to navigating through wilderness seasons of obscurity is a willingness to focus on what you can do for yourself, and what you can change in you.

The bottom line is that none of us are perfect, and because you're working to restore life to the blessing God intended, doesn't mean you've failed. It means there is a blessed life up ahead.

USING THIS WORKBOOK

Each session of your workbook will include chapter summaries, fill in the blank and discussion questions. We've also included key Scripture from each chapter to center your focus on the topic.

We've included video teaching sessions streamed from a secure online environment. The sessions directly correspond with the content in this workbook. As you watch each message, you can follow along with the teaching outline in your workbook.

QUESTIONS

This section of your workbook features fill-in-the blank and multiple-choice questions to help you review key themes from the teaching. Some questions will immediately invoke a memory or emotion. Don't suppress it. Allow yourself to process feelings you may not even realize you're still dealing with.

Other questions may even bring some tension or frustration to the surface. This is normal. When needed, take a break and revisit the questions later. Be committed to the process of working through this guide. Trust that the end result will be a better, more blessed you.

Session One

Identifying Obscurity (Chapter One)

DISCUSSION

Going through seasons in the wilderness isn't easy. It wasn't meant to be easy. Actually, obscurity is intended to prepare you for God's next anointing while also allowing you to address issues currently in your life that may be preventing forward progress.

> *But we all, with unveiled face, beholding as in a mirror the glory of the Lord, are being transformed into the same image from glory to glory, just as by the Spirit of the Lord.*
>
> 2 Corinthians 3:18 (NKJV)

Our lives are created for change as we develop physically, emotionally and spiritually. The process of growth and preparation requires the cycles of obscurity for identifying areas in your life requiring healing, forgiving or committing. Although obscurity can become a dark season when you feel God has stepped aside, it is not meant to punish, but prepare.

> *Submit yourselves, then, to God. Resist the devil, and he will flee from you.*
>
> James 4:7 New International Version (NIV)

Why can't God just bless us, you might ask. That's a great question and we've both asked it too. When we remain within the atmosphere of the natural man, there's a resistance to leave contentment.

> *They are like trees planted along the riverbank, bearing fruit each season.*
>
> *Their leaves never wither, and they prosper in all they do.*
>
> *Psalms 1:3,*
>
> *Christian Standard Bible (CSB)*

We fight against change and unrecognized growth. In other words, we like being cozy where we are. If God didn't get involved, you'd become stagnant, and stagnation stinks!

Because you're experiencing challenging times doesn't mean this is your license to surrender because you feel confused or resentful. You are actually on the verge of moving from glory to glory, so hang in there because transformation is His goal.

Lesson One

Fill in the blanks from Adam & Scott's teaching taken from Chapter 1:

1. Although obscurity is an oddly negative sounding term, it in fact presents the opportunity for _____transformational_____ change.

2. Seasons of obscurity is a cyclical phenomenon designed to progress us along the path of our life's _____trajectory_____.

3. Even if it's destructive, we're naturally _____resistant_____ to abandon contentment because we prefer the ease of the known and comfortable.

4. Entire seasons of obscurity without _____purpose_____, vision or guidance may actually lead to serious issues of melancholy, loneliness, depression and potentially suicide ideation.

5. Finding ourselves in a season of obscurity usually comes without _____warning_____.

6. One of the most common seasons of obscurity we all face is the double-edged sword of obeying God's _____call_____ for our life.

7. No one wants the _____burden_____ of feeling alone, unwanted and unloved.

8. The tricky thing about most of our seasons of obscurity is that those feelings exist only within your _____perception_____ of the times.

9. This is not your _____license_____ to surrender because you feel confused or resentful.

10. It's actually in the separation we experience when feeling "below" life's surface that the true nutrients for _____change_____ are found.

ADDITIONAL NOTES FROM LESSON ONE

Take this opportunity to pray over and think about what was shared in this lesson. Reading is informational but meditating over what was read becomes transformational. Write out your thoughts, observations and questions that may have come up during the lesson. Go back through the chapter or keep this on hand as your work through the book. The time you invest in prayer will also reveal the answers or clarity that you may seek for very personal questions.

DISCUSSION QUESTIONS

1. Write out in detail your memory of the moment you first realized you were in a wilderness season of obscurity. Once you've written in detail, meditate over what you recall versus what you first perceived as it was happening and identify inconsistent incidents that may still be causing confusion, stress or pain.

_____
_____
_____
_____
_____
_____
_____
_____

2. Have you experienced transformational changes in your life as a result of persevering through a wilderness season of obscurity? If so, write out in detail what it was that God changed in your life. If you broke off old chains. how are you changed and better prepared for your new anointing?

_____
_____
_____

VIDEO TEACHING

Our video covers Lesson 1, and we want you to think through what you read and heard. As we've discussed the meaning and ability to identify obscurity, what were your thoughts? How does your experience relate or differ? Write out your thoughts, fears, victories and faith that God has in your future. (videos accessed at *https://www.favorednotforgotten.com*)

Session Two

Transformational Opportunities (Chapter Two)

DISCUSSION

Remember the saying "If I could go back in time but still know what I know now?" Well, thanks to the cycles of obscurity we'll experience, you'll get that opportunity. Sort of, but the idea of moving through these seasons is to lay a solid foundation before moving up.

When the next supernatural elevation comes around, you have all of the previous transformational lessons constructed beneath you to support your newest assignment.

Change can be tough, and positive growth occurs as a result of the tough times. Could you imagine stepping into center court at Wimbledon without ever having held a tennis racket? Your opponent would be licking their chops to destroy you.

> *Then the word of the Lord came to Elijah: "Leave here, turn eastward and hide in the Kerith Ravine, east of the Jordan. You will drink from the brook, and I have directed the ravens to supply you with food there."*
>
> *So he did what the Lord had told him. He went to the Kerith Ravine, east of the Jordan, and stayed there. The ravens brought him bread and meat in the morning and bread and meat in the evening, and he drank from the brook.*
>
> *1 Kings 17: 2-6*

> *For I know the plans I have for you, declares the Lord, plans for welfare and not for evil, to give you a future and a hope.*
>
> Jeremiah 29:11 (ESV)

Without God's seasons of preparation, you'd experience the very same defeat in real life. But, with training, coaching, practice and competition, you'd elevate your game.

Some people say they don't want to change because they like the life they're currently in, or that they are afraid of the unknown ushered in by change. First of all, God did not give us a spirit of fear, and next, not wanting to change because you feel like you've found peace doesn't mean that the temporary absence of chaos is God's rest. Remain vibrant and open to understanding that this is a time for preparing you to receive God's blessing.

Lesson Two

Fill in the blanks from Adam & Scott's teaching taken from Chapter 2:

1. Moving from old seasons to new seasons while retaining the ___knowledge___ and wisdom from every prior phase is a blessing.

2. It's usually because of your ___finances___, and career or personal status that you feel like the world is crumbling beneath you.

3. Although it may feel as though God has completely abandoned you, there cannot be transformation in you as long as you're holding onto ___status quo___.

4. Grasping desperately onto the ties that ___bind___ you to where you are will not free you to move into where He wants you to be.

5. Obscurity is a reason to rejoice because each season is actually providing transformational ___opportunities___.

6. God's ___protection___ in obscurity allowed Jesus's anointing to become refined until it was time to activate it with his baptism.

7. Spiritual growth occurs not by chronological age but through ___supernatural___ maturation.

8. Adam lists three transformational opportunities in obscurity: __freedom__ from pressures to perform, time to __reinvent__ yourself, time to __replenish__ yourself.

9. Scott shared: While still enduring difficulty, my __struggles__ became less as my __reliance__ became more.

10. This is a time of blessing you with __healing__, breaking off strongholds that have and will hold you down and __gifting__ you with new supernatural skills needed for the next phase in your life's journey.

ADDITIONAL NOTES FROM LESSON TWO

Take this opportunity to pray over and think about what was shared in this lesson. Reading is informational but meditating over what was read becomes transformational. Write out your thoughts, observations and questions that may have come up during the lesson. Go back through the chapter or keep this on hand as your work through the book. The time you invest in prayer will also reveal the answers or clarity that you may seek for very personal questions.

DISCUSSION QUESTIONS

1. Do you feel like God abandoned you in your wilderness season? Is there anger or resentment toward Him or anyone else because of the intensity of the transformational process? Sometimes people feel the means did not justify the ends or that what they lost in the way of personal, professional, financial or influential equity was too much. It is okay to have these feelings, but it's vital that you explore why they persist. Describe what it is that causes these feelings, why it still persists, and what your heart is telling you about why it is you went through the transformational process.

_____

_____

_____

_____

_____

_____

_____

_____

2. Have you experienced a new you after the supernatural process of a wilderness season of obscurity? Are you closer to God as a result? Do you feel as though His anointing and plans for you are clearly laid out and understood? Detail what you understand those changes to be and how they have defined you today as opposed to who you were before entering

obscurity. Include what you understand as the new anointing and calling in your life.

_____
_____
_____
_____
_____
_____
_____
_____

VIDEO TEACHING

Our video covers Lesson 2, and we want you to think through what you read and heard. As we've discussed the meaning and ability to identify obscurity, what were your thoughts? How does your experience relate or differ? Write out your thoughts, fears, victories and faith that God has in your future. (videos accessed at *https://www.favorednotforgotten.com*)

_____
_____
_____
_____

Session Three

COST of Obscurity (Chapter Three)

DISCUSSION

This chapter is the heart of what we're sharing with you, so please give Chapter 3 the time and attention it deserves. Wilderness seasons of obscurity are not something the general public has access to.

It's not a self-help or DIY project. This is God-ordained, Holy Spirit led transformation from the person you used to be into the new creation God has ordained you to become. But guess what? It doesn't come without a price to be paid.

> *For which of you, desiring to build a tower, does not first sit down and count the cost, whether he has enough to complete it? Otherwise, when he has laid a foundation and is not able to finish, all who see it begin to mock him, saying, 'This man began to build and was not able to finish.'*
>
> Luke 14:28-30 (ESV)

> *Let your eyes look directly forward and your gaze be straight before you.*
>
> *Ponder the path of your feet; then all your ways will be sure.*
>
> *Do not swerve to the right or to the left turn your foot away from evil.*
>
> Proverbs 4:25-27 (ESV)

God has already paid the ultimate price through the sacrifice of His son, Jesus, on the cross, but there is a cost you too must count as a condition of walking in God's light for your life.

The challenges presented through wilderness seasons are part of that cost. We've created

> *Beloved, do not believe every spirit, but test the spirits to see whether they are from God, for many false prophets have gone out into the world. By this you know the Spirit of God: every spirit that confesses that Jesus Christ has come in the flesh is from God, and every spirit that does not confess Jesus is not from God. This is the spirit of the antichrist, which you heard was coming and now is in the world already.*
>
> 1 John 4 (ESV)

an illustration, aptly named COST (Calling, Obscurity, Stabilization, Transformation) to share each of what we believe are the keys to proclaiming God's blessings.

While each is detailed in the book, it's important to understand each phase as they have and will relate to your journey through the wilderness. What we found most challenging and often derails people at the very beginning is the calling.

We usually think that when God calls us out that our path had been paved and it's time to bask in the joy of His presence. Except that's not always the case when preparing us for higher kingdom service.

Just like Moses, Jesus and Paul among others, we are called by God and then ushered away for our own protection until we've broken off anything from our past that prevents our elevation in the future.

Unfortunately, during those times, we may feel abandoned by God or begin to question whether we heard Him correctly.

This is the transitional phase between calling and obscurity. We've walked you through those two and the others so you can have the assurance that God has not left you or is punishing you. To the contrary, He's preparing to bless you with an incredible anointing.

Lesson Three

Fill in the blanks from Adam & Scott's teaching taken from Chapter 3:

1. The consequences for fully investing in __Christ__ can cost the very relationships within your earthly family for example, but __Jesus__ doesn't force us to take that action.

2. During the __calling__, it's not uncommon to get lost in the haze of the band's blast with the deafening silence of __misunderstanding__.

3. When we become aware of the calling, the only way to activate the fresh anointing is through your act of __obedience__.

4. Understanding that Obscurity is only for our personal growth, maturity and new opportunities, it's still __taxing__.

5. A consideration about journeying through wilderness seasons is that there are no prescribed __times__ for moving into and out of the __cycles__.

6. There is light at the end of the tunnel, and just before you're able to grab a big old handful of brightness, comes a period of __stabilization__.

7. It is during the time of Stabilization that we begin questioning the __value__ of worldly things and life as we're living it.

8. Arriving at the point of being stable in your season of obscurity is also when you first feel like you're beginning to catch _____traction_____ against circumstances that left you helplessly slipping through uncertain _____terrain_____.

9. Actualizing the full effect of transformation requires an active _____acceptance_____ for the gifts God has imparted in you during this time as well as a _____grateful_____ heart for the strongholds broken off of your life.

10. Your new _____you_____ has been prepared by God the Father, but ultimately it is your _____choice_____ whether to accept or reject the activation of His anointing.

ADDITIONAL NOTES FROM LESSON THREE

Take this opportunity to pray over and think about what was shared in this lesson. Reading is informational but meditating over what was read becomes transformational. Write out your thoughts, observations and questions that may have come up during the lesson. Go back through the chapter or keep this on hand as your work through the book. The time you invest in prayer will also reveal the answers or clarity that you may seek for very personal questions.

DISCUSSION QUESTIONS

1. How accurate were the stages of COST as they related to your season of wilderness? If you experienced chaos or doubt after the clarity of Calling, when and how did it return to knowing you had first heard God speak clearly? Describe what was going on inside as you shifted from the possible excitement of your Calling and the possible darkness of your Obscurity.

_____
_____
_____
_____
_____
_____
_____
_____

2. The first two stages of wilderness journeys have the high potential for creating confusion in our lives but coming into an atmosphere of Stabilization is the true beginning of realizing your new anointing. Describe at what stage or time in your process did you first understand that your feet were on solid ground. If your emotions toward God were murky through the darker times, when did the fog begin to clear? How did that help restore your faith?

_____
_____
_____
_____
_____
_____
_____
_____
_____

3. What did your Transformation stage look like? Do you feel you'd received God's full anointing? Were you willing to fully embrace all that God wanted to work out of and into your life? What are you currently doing to continue fulfilling God's will for your life and future?

_____
_____
_____
_____
_____
_____
_____
_____

VIDEO TEACHING

Our video covers Lesson 3, and we want you to think through what you read and heard. As we've discussed the meaning and ability to identify obscurity, what were your thoughts? How does your experience relate or differ? Write out your thoughts, fears, victories and faith that God has in your future. (videos accessed at *https://www.favorednotforgotten.com*)

_____
_____
_____
_____
_____
_____
_____
_____
_____

Session Four

Obscurity in the Bible (Chapter Four)

DISCUSSION

Every single thing we want to know about in this life is found in the greatest love letter and instruction manual ever written. It should come as no surprise when our lives have seemed to crumble into a trail of broken promises and unrealized expectations that God's

> *And we know that in all things God works for the good of those who love him, who have been called according to his purpose.*
>
> Romans 8:28

> *3 As he neared Damascus on his journey, suddenly a light from heaven flashed around him. 4 He fell to the ground and heard a voice say to him, "Saul, Saul, why do you persecute me?" 5 "Who are you, Lord?" Saul asked. "I am Jesus, whom you are persecuting," he replied. 6 "Now get up and go into the city, and you will be told what you must do."*
>
> Acts 9:3-6 (NIV)

Word has not only the answers but also tangible examples.

Do you think you're the only one who has walked in obscurity? I bet until you read this book you thought you were. You are not alone, and if our personal examples aren't enough to help set your feet back on solid rock, we want to share the experiences of Moses, Jesus and Paul. How do you feel about being in their company?

> *And a voice from heaven said, "This is my Son, whom I love; with him I am well pleased."*
>
> *Matthew 3:17 (NIV)*

As you read through each of these heroes from our history, you will see that they too moved through wilderness season as we applied the COST (calling, obscurity, stabilization & transformation) model. Were these brothers blessed by God the Father? Yes, they were extremely blessed upon exiting their obscurity experiences and you will be too.

Lesson Four

Fill in the blanks from Adam & Scott's teaching taken from Chapter 4:

1. Obscurity isn't a modern __self-help__ idea that's useful for explaining why we go through __tough__ times. It's as old as time itself, as vital today in shaping your __life__ as it was back then.

2. Moses only came to understand that direction after he lived out his transformation through __obscurity__.

3. Moses's early life created an identity __crisis__ that would bring pain into his life.

4. It's common during seasons of obscurity for God to send a __Jethro__ into your life to provide additional support for moving the rest of the way in your __journey__.

5. Paul's calling to __Christ__ is quick, fast, unexpected and __radical__.

6. Eventually, even Paul's closest __friends__ failed to come check on him, and __obscurity__ became a very lonely place.

7. Despite the extreme __hardships__ and danger, Paul understood the __purpose__ of what he'd

been through and the value for what he'd produce. It was during this season that the _____ Prison Epistles _____ are written.

8. _____ Jesus's _____ life on this earth was purely because of His _____ calling _____.

9. Jesus's first season of _____ obscurity _____ prepared him for _____ ministry _____ that occurred immediately after he received the power of the Holy Spirit and his Father's _____ affirmation _____ of his identity.

10. _____ Transformation _____ is the full circle that began when God first placed His _____ desire _____ in your heart through a calling to serve.

ADDITIONAL NOTES FROM LESSON FOUR

Take this opportunity to pray over and think about what was shared in this lesson. Reading is informational but meditating over what was read becomes transformational. Write out your thoughts, observations and questions that may have come up during the lesson. Go back through the chapter or keep this on hand as your work through the book. The time you invest in prayer will also reveal the answers or clarity that you may seek for very personal questions.

DISCUSSION QUESTIONS

1. Does it help to see actual, historical examples of the COST model overlaid in the lives of biblical heroes? Does it also provide you with a true sense of connection in knowing that you have shared a transformative experience just like they did? Explain those feelings as they help connect you to your wilderness season and your path toward kingdom service.

_____

_____

_____

_____

_____

_____

_____

_____

2. We purposefully relied on the examples of Moses, Jesus and Paul because they also give us very different salvation experiences. Actually, anyone from the Bible could have illustrated their wilderness season as it applied to the COST model. We love how Moses came to receive his calling over many years, while Jesus was actually born to serve, and Paul received the radical transformation of salvation. Which one most resembles your faith journey?

VIDEO TEACHING

Our video covers Lesson 4, and we want you to think through what you read and heard. As we've discussed the meaning and ability to identify obscurity, what were your thoughts? How does your experience relate or differ? Write out your thoughts, fears, victories and faith that God has in your future. (videos accessed at *https://www.favorednotforgotten.com*)

Session Five

Obscuring Our Deepest Needs (Chapter Five)

DISCUSSION

Let's get into the core of who we are and why we do what we do. I know we can spend years exploring and fortunes uncovering the answers to this, but it's simple and like all questions about life, the answers are found in the Bible.

> *Then God said, "Let us make mankind in our image, in our likeness…*
>
> *Genesis 1:26 (NIV)*

God created us out of His nature and His nature is love. He cannot act beyond that nature because He is love. That would be like you deciding to be a rabbit. You can hop around and eat yuckie carrots all day, but you cannot ever be a rabbit. So, stop eating those carrots!

In His loving nature as creator, we were fashioned. All living things have a desire to know their creator. God's initial plan was to enjoy a super up close and personal relationship with us.

> *So we have come to know and to believe the love that God has for us. God is love, and whoever abides in love abides in God, and God abides in him.*
>
> *1 John 4:16 ESV*

Look at the way He lived with Adam and Eve. In that intimacy, He fulfilled all of their needs. Even the deepest ones: love, security, significance and purpose. They were meant to be an internal provision as only God could supply.

> *And you will feel secure, because there is hope; you will look around and take your rest in security.*
>
> *Job 11:18 ESV*

Well, as sin goes, our direct connection to our loving Father was severed and so was the internal satisfaction in having our deepest needs met. Once man had fallen because of the selfish desire to satisfy self, the four deepest needs became an external pursuit. Since only God can completely fill what only He created, our need for love, security, significance and purpose cannot be completely satisfied on our own.

Wilderness seasons of obscurity amplify our realization that we are absent of what we desire most. First is the intimate relationship with God the Father and as a result of that longing, so goes our gratification of feeling loved, having security, being significant and having a purpose.

Make no mistake, this is not a time of punishment and God has not abandoned you. As a matter of fact, He's never been closer because He does indeed love you, provides security for you, makes you significant because you are His, and fills your life of purpose because you live for Him.

> *What do you think? If a man has a hundred sheep, and one of them has gone astray, does he not leave the ninety-nine on the mountains and go in search of the one that went astray?*
>
> *Matthew 18:12 (ESV)*

Lesson Five

Fill in the blanks from Adam & Scott's teaching taken from Chapter 5:

1. When the _____Bible_____ says to glorify Him, it is only out of His _____love_____ that we were created, and for love that we remain.

2. In creating us, God imparted four needs deep into our temple where the _____Holy_____ _____Spirit_____ resides.

3. He provided for their internal needs of _____love_____, _____security_____, _____significance_____ and _____purpose_____.

4. Christ's _____ascension_____ (Acts 1) provided for the Holy Spirit's arrival for the purpose of activating our _____anointed_____ relationship with God the Father.

5. Because God is love, the relationship with Him is based on the highest form of love – _____agape_____.

6. _____Obscurity_____ can cause us to feel like love is _____absent_____, but the truth is, it was love that sent us into the season because God loves us.

7. If we're going to experience spiritual _____breakthrough_____, then there are gifts and activations of your anointing that must be received through God's _____gift_____.

8. As a child of God, we are so much more _____ significant _____ than what we drive or what others refer to us on our job. We are kings and _____ priests _____.

9. It's not uncommon prior to receiving your _____ calling _____ to actually be in a place where you are fully enjoying the fruits of your actualized _____ purpose _____.

10. It's okay to _____ struggle _____ over the initial loss of seeing your life's purpose with vibrant _____ clarity _____ for a season. God will light your path when where you've been is no longer what _____ satisfies _____ your deepest needs.

ADDITIONAL NOTES FROM LESSON FIVE

Take this opportunity to pray over and think about what was shared in this lesson. Reading is informational but meditating over what was read becomes transformational. Write out your thoughts, observations and questions that may have come up during the lesson. Go back through the chapter or keep this on hand as your work through the book. The time you invest in prayer will also reveal the answers or clarity that you may seek for very personal questions.

DISCUSSION QUESTIONS

1. Write out what makes you feel most loved, gives you a sense of security, makes you feel significant and where do you find your purpose. Explore the potential that your answers might have changed since experiencing a wilderness season of obscurity.

_____

_____

_____

_____

_____

_____

_____

_____

_____

2. Your season of obscurity is meant for transformational change that prepares you for a new anointing but most importantly, draws you into a closer understanding of God the Father. Try to articulate where you were in your faith walk in regards to intimacy of connection as compared to where you are post-obscurity journey.

_____

_____

_____

VIDEO TEACHING

Our video covers Lesson 5, and we want you to think through what you read and heard. As we've discussed the meaning and ability to identify obscurity, what were your thoughts? How does your experience relate or differ? Write out your thoughts, fears, victories and faith that God has in your future. (videos accessed at *https://www.favorednotforgotten.com*)

Session Six

The Choice of Fear or Faith (Chapter Six)

DISCUSSION

People can be tough to read. You tell them they have to do something, and they get upset and withdraw into this entitled bubble of independence. On the other hand, let them know they have a choice but must choose wisely and they are insulted because you left them hanging to make a big decision.

> *"He brought us out from there in order to bring us in, to give us the land which He had sworn to our fathers"*
>
> Deuteronomy 6:23 (KJV)

But guess what? God's gift of free will does exactly that. He loves us so much that He leaves us to make our own choice where it comes to having a relationship with Him or not.

A daily choice we must make is to live a life of fear or faith. Not making a decision is still making a choice. There is no neutral ground in this situation, and avoidance is akin to fear.

We love referencing 2 Timothy 1:7, because God tells us why living in fear is not spiritual. We simply were not given a fearful spirit, and therefore if we choose to live in fear, what we have ultimately chosen to do is live outside the will of God and reside in the darkness of being afraid. Now this doesn't mean we have

> *Now faith is the substance of things hoped for, the evidence of things not seen*
>
> Hebrews 11:1 (KJV)

> *"The land we passed through and explored is exceedingly good. If the Lord is pleased with us, he will lead us into that land, a land flowing with milk and honey, and will give it to us. Only do not rebel against the Lord. And do not be afraid of the people of the land, because we will devour them. Their protection is gone, but the Lord is with us. Do not be afraid of them."*
>
> Numbers 14:7-9

to be daredevils who jump from planes, trains and bridges, but it does mean we live with a spirit of power, love and self-control.

Seasons of obscurity are helpful for breaking off whatever chains keep you shackled to your past. The reality is, there is freedom on the other side when you willingly embrace the new anointing, but God is not going to force you to accept His gift, no more than He'll force you to accept His son, Jesus. That's how much He loves you. So, when it comes to choosing fear or faith, know that in faith, you are not alone.

Lesson Six

Fill in the blanks from Adam & Scott's teaching taken from Chapter 6:

1. Understanding that obscurity is not a __punishment__ but a gift in waiting, you should also understand God isn't forcing you into this season.

2. __Times__ change and even if you had clung to a post within safe harbor, storms would still __rage__, waters would still rise, and winds would still howl.

3. Had we not entered into an __atmosphere__ of feeding our good wolf, there would've been the prolonged __consequence__ of faithless disobedience similar to that of God's people as they were poised to enter His Promised Land.

4. In much the same way God called you out, He also makes a promise to __protect__ and __provide__ for you.

5. Although there was an ironclad __assurance__ of a better life in an environment created by God himself, the __Israelites__ stumbled in their obedience and faith walk.

6. Let's commit to taking our __shoes__ off on the holy ground of this God encountered obscurity because this choice determines whether you are a __grasshopper__ or giant killer.

48

7. Despite the fact that the land was the way God described it as _____flowing_____ with milk and honey, they _____feared_____ the inhabitants.

8. _____Fear_____ requires a choice to allow yourself to be directed by strong and unpleasant _____emotions_____.

9. We also understand that obscurity brings our fears to the _____surface_____ because it's only within these seasons that we're no longer _____tethered_____ to the safety straps of what it was we once knew.

10. If you want deeper _____waters_____ to withstand life's storms, you first must go through the _____storms_____ of deep waters.

ADDITIONAL NOTES FROM LESSON SIX

Take this opportunity to pray over and think about what was shared in this lesson. Reading is informational but meditating over what was read becomes transformational. Write out your thoughts, observations and questions that may have come up during the lesson. Go back through the chapter or keep this on hand as your work through the book. The time you invest in prayer will also reveal the answers or clarity that you may seek for very personal questions.

DISCUSSION QUESTIONS

1. Prior to and at the beginning of your wilderness season of obscurity, were there areas in your life where fear kept you from taking that leap? How about when you first heard God's calling for your new direction, did that cause you to hesitate or maybe you simply ignored it. Describe areas of fear that served as strongholds in your life.

_____
_____
_____
_____
_____
_____
_____
_____

2. Have you been able to look back to identify areas of fear that held you back from living a blessed life as God intended? What has been the change to where you are now? Meditate on areas that may still have hooks into your spirit and focus on severing those tethers.

_____
_____
_____

VIDEO TEACHING

Our video covers Lesson 6, and we want you to think through what you read and heard. As we've discussed the meaning and ability to identify obscurity, what were your thoughts? How does your experience relate or differ? Write out your thoughts, fears, victories and faith that God has in your future. (videos accessed at *https://www.favorednotforgotten.com*)

Session Seven

Crossing the Bridge of Obscurity (Chapter Seven)

DISCUSSION

The illustration of crossing a bridge ties in so beautifully with the previous chapter about choosing fear or faith. Did you know there are some bridges in this world that people are horrified to cross? Some people actually hire drivers to transport them in their own vehicle across bridges that scare them. And still, some people decide to simply camp out on one side and never attempt to cross the divide. This is what we want to focus on in this session.

Traveling along your journey through the wilderness of obscurity will require several major crossing benchmarks. Maybe it'll come to forgiving an abuser who left you with scars that have prevented you from having a normal relationship with your spouse, or a dominant parent who forced you to perform for their approval. Maybe your

> "whoever wants to become great among you must be your servant, and whoever wants to be first must be your slave—just as the Son of Man did not come to be served, but to serve, and to give his life as a ransom for many."
>
> Matthew 20:26-28

> "Consider it pure joy, my brothers and sisters, whenever you face trials of many kinds, because you know that the testing of your faith produces perseverance. Let perseverance finish its work so that you may be mature and complete, not lacking anything."
>
> James 1:2-4

> *"I know what it is to be in need, and I know what it is to have plenty. I have learned the secret of being content in any and every situation, whether well fed or hungry, whether living in plenty or in want."*
>
> Philippians 4:12

bridge crossing sign says something about giving up on your worldly dreams and serving others above yourself. Some people refuse to cross bridges that simply ask you to serve God.

No one is going to shove you onto that bridge and make you cross it. That's up to you, but the only way you'll exit the tough times of the wilderness journey is by crossing that bridge. There are blessings waiting for you on the other side, and just like Jesus was tended to by angels when His forty days of being tempted by satan was completed, God is comforting you right now. All you have to do is loosen your strangle hold on the railings and move toward Him.

Lesson Seven

Fill in the blanks from Adam & Scott's teaching taken from Chapter 7:

1. While seasons of obscurity may launch with __obedience__ to God's calling, the experience once within the cycle becomes unexpected and often filled with struggle.

2. That action involves crossings that once completed can __never__ return you to the person you once were prior to that action.

3. Obscurity is the tool God uses to develop __character__ in our lives that cannot be developed any other way.

4. The desire for greatness is within us, but the world has an __upside-down__ ideology regarding fame and fortune.

5. Times of obscurity are designed to bring us into __maturity__, to tenderize our hearts with the kind of humility required to experience success and not fall prey to __pride__.

6. If we don't __embrace__ the season of obscurity, we won't be prepared for our season of __influence__.

7. You need to cross that bridge if you feel like you need to __embellish__ or exaggerate your __life__.

8. Sometimes others' _____ (opinions) or disapproval can make us question the voice of God in our lives.

9. The trial of obscurity teaches us _____ (dependence) on God; it increases our faith and develops integrity; we learn contentment, endurance, patience and _____ (humility).

10. You do not have to seek out _____ (significance). The glory of _____ (victory) will find you.

ADDITIONAL NOTES FROM LESSON SEVEN

Take this opportunity to pray over and think about what was shared in this lesson. Reading is informational but meditating over what was read becomes transformational. Write out your thoughts, observations and questions that may have come up during the lesson. Go back through the chapter or keep this on hand as your work through the book. The time you invest in prayer will also reveal the answers or clarity that you may seek for very personal questions.

DISCUSSION QUESTIONS

1. Describe in tangible terms what are the most pressing issues that have or will cause to struggle with cross the bridge of obscurity? If you have already crossed, describe your feelings of having made that part of the journey.

_____

_____

_____

_____

_____

_____

_____

_____

_____

2. Have you lost influence as you ventured into your journey? Did the experience make you believe that maybe even your message was no longer relevant, and that you had lost the anointed calling God once ordained you with? Detail how that made you feel and explain what steps you did to compensate for that season. If you've come through, describe the reality of why you felt that way and where you are in your perception of spiritual influence and message.

_____

_____

VIDEO TEACHING

Our video covers Lesson 7, and we want you to think through what you read and heard. As we've discussed the meaning and ability to identify obscurity, what were your thoughts? How does your experience relate or differ? Write out your thoughts, fears, victories and faith that God has in your future. (videos accessed at *https://www.favorednotforgotten.com*)

Session Eight

Thriving In Obscurity and The New You (Chapter Eight)

DISCUSSION

It's always a relief to get to this final session where we can discuss the concept of thriving. Your journey has been tough, maybe it's driven you right to the very edge of personal, financial and professional destruction. Was the rope you once clung to reduced to a thread? We've shared from the beginning that wilderness seasons of obscurity are God's charted course for growing you in His influence. Thriving is the best way we can describe it. Maybe it does mean regaining what was lost, but in reality, whatever was pruned from your life as a direct result of obscurity needed to be let loose because it was contributing to your being chained to the past.

> *And whatever you do, in word or deed, do everything in the name of the Lord Jesus, giving thanks to God the Father through him.*
>
> Colossians 3:17 (ESV)

Having rolled up to the top of obscurity's cycle, it is good to see things crystal clearly. But beware that some people who've just stepped out of their COST model are still struggling to articulate

> *And Samuel said, "Has the Lord as great delight in burnt offerings and sacrifices, as in obeying the voice of the Lord? Behold, to obey is better than sacrifice, and to listen than the fat of rams.*
>
> 1 Samuel 15:22 ESV

> *For if anyone thinks he is something, when he is nothing, he deceives himself.*
>
> Galatians 6:3 ESV

what it was that just happened to their life. We shared that Scott had not been able to categorize what it was he'd gone through although he understood God's work in his life. Adam, who had previously walked out his obscurity journey helped Scott by giving him the anchor word that flipped the light switch on—obscurity.

You will thrive once you've completed the journey, had the time to take stock in what you'd just experienced and learned to wait patiently on the Lord to order your next steps. You've been through God's very own process for advancing His beloved in the preparation for receiving a new, fresh anointing. You must be made the vessel to receive what He is waiting to pour into you. Remaining vulnerable for the adventure expedites your readiness to receive. We are so excited to see what God will do in your life!

> *But seek first the kingdom of God and his righteousness, and all these things will be added to you.*
>
> Matthew 6:33 (ESV)

Lesson Eight

Fill in the blanks from Adam & Scott's teaching taken from Chapter 8:

1. Unfortunately, each of us experiencing seasons of obscurity find no _____ (solace) in comparing the trials of each other to what means the most to us.

2. It's not surprising to hear people share that they feel alone or _____ (abandoned), but in order for God to do his work in your life requires the _____ (potter) to go directly hands on with the clay.

3. Thriving in your walk begins with acknowledging that God is in _____ (charge).

4. The first and most important influencing factor is your _____ (attitude).

5. A big part of why we find ourselves in cycles of obscurity is thanks in part to our stubborn resistance to God's will and _____ (authority).

6. The typical Western response to the subject of obedience is one of _____ (resistance) because of a connotation to defeatism or _____ (subjugation).

7. Don't abandon your _____ (willingness) to obey God's prompting through the Holy Spirit.

8. Developing your _____Christ-character_____ sets a solid foundation upon which God begins building a new, improved you.

9. It's understandable if you're simply _____unaware_____ or misinformed, but to know better and fail to do better is a really _____self-destructive_____ position within which to operate.

10. Show us your _____friends_____ and we'll show you your _____future_____.

ADDITIONAL NOTES FROM LESSON EIGHT

Take this opportunity to pray over and think about what was shared in this lesson. Reading is informational but meditating over what was read becomes transformational. Write out your thoughts, observations and questions that may have come up during the lesson. Go back through the chapter or keep this on hand as your work through the book. The time you invest in prayer will also reveal the answers or clarity that you may seek for very personal questions.

DISCUSSION QUESTIONS

1. Thriving in obscurity involves a huge emphasis on character development. Our character defines who we are, how we behave and who we most desire to be. List out characteristics of your character before you began your wilderness season of obscurity and compare or contrast traits you now identify.

_____
_____
_____
_____
_____
_____
_____
_____

2. Divine alignments are a big part of moving closer to God's heart because it's a direct relationship to other people. Are your friends believers? Do you hang out with people based on your job or who can do something special for you? Describe the type of friend you are to others, and if you've moved through obscurity, make sure to detail any changes in the type of company you keep and what your relationship to them is.

_____
_____

3. Finally, congratulations and thank you for working through this workbook. Looking at the big picture of your life at this very moment, how are you?

VIDEO TEACHING

Our video covers Lesson 8, and we want you to think through what you read and heard. As we've discussed the meaning and ability to identify obscurity, what were your thoughts? How does your experience relate or differ? Write out your thoughts, fears, victories and faith that God has in your future. (videos accessed at *https://www.favorednotforgotten.com*)

About Pastor Adam McCain

Pastor Adam McCain is a passionate follower of Jesus Christ. Happily married to his college sweetheart, Jami, they have three amazing kids and serve as the Lead Pastors of Church on the Hill in Cedar Hill, Texas. Adam began serving in full-time pastoral ministry at age 19, spending the first decade growing a revolutionary small groups-based youth ministry at a mega-church in Louisiana, where he and Jami first met. Today, they continue to support each other's callings, both Adam's teaching and preaching gift and Jami's skill for creating positive community change through her political influence.

After decades of being a headline speaker at national and international ministry events, Adam is best known for engaging audiences with his real-talk Biblical wisdom and one-of-a-kind storytelling. Adam's calling is to raise up global leaders who are equipped to impact their communities by daily living out the doing-life-together and discipleship-making Gospel of Jesus Christ.

In 2001, Adam became the Director at Christ for the Nations Institute (CFNI). During the seven years of his directorship, the school experienced unprecedented growth and launched countless ministry leaders who are still serving churches around the world today. He continues to be a sought-after speaker there, including regularly teaching his course on Personal Discipleship.

In addition, Adam and Jami together provide mentorship and development to local pastors and their wives through the Global Ministers Network

(GMN). From all ages and stages of life, Adam and Jami connect with these pastors regularly to encourage each other, share resources and continue strengthening their skills in the challenging and rewarding work of leading people deeper with Jesus. Over the past 10 years, Adam and Jami have mentored dozens of pastors who have reached 1000s of people through their services and special events.

Since 2005, Adam and Jami have given their hearts to serving as the Founding and Lead Pastors of Church on the Hill, a thriving small groups-based church centrally located in Cedar Hill, Texas, with a second campus in Mansfield, Texas. A significant number of the founding leaders they began with continue to serve in leadership even today -- a testimony to the kind of lifestyle and life-long pastoring the McCains champion and embody so well.

About Dr. Scott Silverii

Scott is a son of the Living God. Thankful for the gift of his wife, Leah, they share seven kids combined. Career law enforcement until God called him into His service, Scott promptly retired as a Chief of Police and entered into ministry. He's certified through MarriageToday as a Marriage On The Rock counselor and a SYMBIS facilitator.

The "Chief" admits what he thought he'd learned from leading others during a highly decorated career that included 12 years undercover and 16 years in SWAT, was nothing like leading people to Christ.

Currently in seminary studies pursuing a Doctor of Ministry, Scott has earned a Master of Public Administration and a Ph.D. in Cultural Anthropology. Education and experience have allowed for a deeper understanding in ministering to the wounded, as he worked to break free from his own past of pain and abuse.

In 2016, Scott was led to plant a church in the third space of digital media. Exclusive to online ministry, Five Stones Church.Online was born out of the calling to combat the negative influences reigning over social media and the demonic effects it has in areas such as pornography, human trafficking, live-streaming violence and the daily diet of corrupted content.

With a global membership, Scott also focuses on law enforcement marriages and men's ministry. Scott's alpha manhood model for today's hero is defined by:

Be on your guard; stand firm in the faith; be courageous; be strong. Do everything in love. (1 Corinthians 16:13-14)

An experienced speaker, mentor and confidential accountability partner, Scott is available for workshops, conferences and churches. Their complete line of resources are at Silverii Ministry.

www.ingramcontent.com/pod-product-compliance
Lightning Source LLC
Chambersburg PA
CBHW082027120526
44592CB00039B/2618